HAL•LEONARD
INSTRUMENTAL
PLAY-ALONG

ALTO SAX

# Andrew Lloyd Webber®
## *Classics*

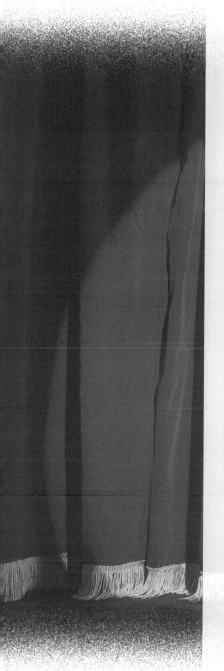

**How To Use The CD Accompaniment:**
A melody cue appears on the right channel only. If your CD player has a balance adjustment, you can adjust the volume of the melody by turning down the right channel.

Andrew Lloyd Webber® is a trademark owned by Andrew Lloyd Webber
Technicolor® is the registered trademark of the Technicolor group of companies.

ISBN 0-634-06155-0

HAL•LEONARD®
CORPORATION
7777 W. BLUEMOUND RD. P.O. BOX 13819 MILWAUKEE, WI 53213

T0052951

Visit Hal Leonard Online at
**www.halleonard.com**

# THE PHANTOM OF THE OPERA
from THE PHANTOM OF THE OPERA

Music by ANDREW LLOYD WEBBER
Lyrics by CHARLES HART
Additional Lyrics by RICHARD STILGOE and MIKE BATT

ALTO SAX

# DON'T CRY FOR ME ARGENTINA

## from EVITA

Words by TIM RICE
Music by ANDREW LLOYD WEBBER

ALTO SAX

# CLOSE EVERY DOOR
from JOSEPH AND THE AMAZING TECHNICOLOR® DREAMCOAT

**CD**

**5**: With melody cue
**6**: Accompaniment only

ALTO SAX

Music by ANDREW LLOYD WEBBER
Lyrics by TIM RICE

# AS IF WE NEVER SAID GOODBYE

from SUNSET BOULEVARD

**CD**

◆**7**: With melody cue
◆**8**: Accompaniment only

**ALTO SAX**

Music by ANDREW LLOYD WEBBER
Lyrics by DON BLACK and CHRISTOPHER HAMPTON,
with contributions by AMY POWERS

# EVERYTHING'S ALRIGHT
## from JESUS CHRIST SUPERSTAR

Words by TIM RICE
Music by ANDREW LLOYD WEBBER

**CD**

◆9 : With melody cue
◆10 : Accompaniment only

ALTO SAX

# GUS: THE THEATRE CAT
## from CATS

Music by ANDREW LLOYD WEBBER
Text by T.S. ELIOT

ALTO SAX

# UNEXPECTED SONG
## from SONG & DANCE

Music by ANDREW LLOYD WEBBER
Lyrics by DON BLACK

ALTO SAX

# THE MUSIC OF THE NIGHT
## from THE PHANTOM OF THE OPERA

Music by ANDREW LLOYD WEBBER
Lyrics by CHARLES HART
Additional Lyrics by RICHARD STILGOE

**CD**
**15** : With melody cue
**16** : Accompaniment only

ALTO SAX

# LOVE CHANGES EVERYTHING
### from ASPECTS OF LOVE

CD
**17**: With melody cue
**18**: Accompaniment only

Music by ANDREW LLOYD WEBBER
Lyrics by DON BLACK and CHARLES HART

ALTO SAX

# WHISTLE DOWN THE WIND
## from WHISTLE DOWN THE WIND

Music by ANDREW LLOYD WEBBER
Lyrics by JIM STEINMAN

**CD**

◆19 : With melody cue
◆20 : Accompaniment only

ALTO SAX

# OUR KIND OF LOVE
from THE BEAUTIFUL GAME

Music by ANDREW LLOYD WEBBER
Lyrics by BEN ELTON

ALTO SAX

# GO GO GO JOSEPH
## from JOSEPH AND THE AMAZING TECHNICOLOR® DREAMCOAT

Music by ANDREW LLOYD WEBBER
Lyrics by TIM RICE

ALTO SAX

# PLAY MORE OF YOUR FAVORITE SONGS

## WITH GREAT INSTRUMENTAL PLAY ALONG PACKS FROM HAL LEONARD

### Ballads

Solo arrangements of 12 songs: Bridge Over Troubled Water • Bring Him Home • Candle in the Wind • Don't Cry for Me Argentina • I Don't Know How to Love Him • Imagine • Killing Me Softly with His Song • Nights in White Satin • Wonderful Tonight • more.

| | | |
|---|---|---|
| 00841445 | Flute | $10.95 |
| 00841446 | Clarinet | $10.95 |
| 00841447 | Alto Sax | $10.95 |
| 00841448 | Tenor Sax | $10.95 |
| 00841449 | Trumpet | $10.95 |
| 00841450 | Trombone | $10.95 |
| 00841451 | Violin | $10.95 |

### Band Jam

12 band favorites complete with accompaniment CD, including: Born to Be Wild • Get Ready for This • I Got You (I Feel Good) • Rock & Roll – Part II (The Hey Song) • Twist and Shout • We Will Rock You • Wild Thing • Y.M.C.A • and more.

| | | |
|---|---|---|
| 00841232 | Flute | $10.95 |
| 00841233 | Clarinet | $10.95 |
| 00841234 | Alto Sax | $10.95 |
| 00841235 | Trumpet | $10.95 |
| 00841236 | Horn | $10.95 |
| 00841237 | Trombone | $10.95 |
| 00841238 | Violin | $10.95 |

### Disney Movie Hits

Now solo instrumentalists can play along with a dozen favorite songs from Disney blockbusters, including: Beauty and the Beast • Circle of Life • Cruella De Vil • Go the Distance • God Help the Outcasts • Kiss the Girl • When She Loved Me • A Whole New World • and more.

| | | |
|---|---|---|
| 00841420 | Flute | $12.95 |
| 00841421 | Clarinet | $12.95 |
| 00841422 | Alto Sax | $12.95 |
| 00841423 | Trumpet | $12.95 |
| 00841424 | French Horn | $12.95 |
| 00841425 | Trombone/Baritone | $12.95 |
| 00841686 | Tenor Sax | $12.95 |
| 00841687 | Oboe | $12.95 |
| 00841688 | Mallet Percussion | $12.95 |
| 00841426 | Violin | $12.95 |
| 00841427 | Viola | $12.95 |
| 00841428 | Cello | $12.95 |

Prices, contents, and availability subject to change without notice. Disney characters and artwork © Disney Enterprises, Inc.

FOR MORE INFORMATION, SEE YOUR LOCAL MUSIC DEALER, OR WRITE TO:

### HAL•LEONARD CORPORATION

7777 W. BLUEMOUND RD. P.O. BOX 13819 MILWAUKEE, WI 53213

Visit Hal Leonard online at **www.halleonard.com**

### Disney Solos

An exciting collection of 12 solos with full-band accompaniment on CD. Songs include: Be Our Guest • Can You Feel the Love Tonight • Colors of the Wind • Reflection • Under the Sea • You've Got a Friend in Me • Zero to Hero • and more.

| | | |
|---|---|---|
| 00841404 | Flute | $12.95 |
| 00841405 | Clarinet/Tenor Sax | $12.95 |
| 00841406 | Alto Sax | $12.95 |
| 00841407 | Horn | $12.95 |
| 00841408 | Trombone | $12.95 |
| 00841409 | Trumpet | $12.95 |
| 00841410 | Violin | $12.95 |
| 00841411 | Viola | $12.95 |
| 00841412 | Cello | $12.95 |
| 00841506 | Oboe | $12.95 |
| 00841553 | Mallet Percussion | $12.95 |

### Easy Disney Favorites

13 Disney favorites for solo instruments: Bibbidi-Bobbidi-Boo • It's a Small World • Let's Go Fly a Kite • Mickey Mouse March • A Spoonful of Sugar • Toyland March • Winnie the Pooh • The Work Song • Zip-A-Dee-Doo-Dah • and many more.

| | | |
|---|---|---|
| 00841371 | Flute | $12.95 |
| 00841477 | Clarinet | $12.95 |
| 00841478 | Alto Sax | $12.95 |
| 00841479 | Trumpet | $12.95 |
| 00841480 | Trombone | $12.95 |
| 00841372 | Violin | $12.95 |
| 00841481 | Viola | $12.95 |
| 00841482 | Cello/Bass | $12.95 |

### Favorite Movie Themes

13 themes, including: *An American Symphony* from Mr. Holland's Opus • Braveheart • Chariots of Fire • Forrest Gump – Main Title • Theme from *Jurassic Park* • Mission: Impossible Theme • and more.

| | | |
|---|---|---|
| 00841166 | Flute | $10.95 |
| 00841167 | Clarinet | $10.95 |
| 00841168 | Trumpet/Tenor Sax | $10.95 |
| 00841169 | Alto Sax | $10.95 |
| 00841170 | Trombone | $10.95 |
| 00841171 | F Horn | $10.95 |
| 00841296 | Violin | $10.95 |

### Jazz & Blues

14 songs: Cry Me a River • Fever • Fly Me to the Moon • God Bless' the Child • Harlem Nocturne • Moonglow • A Night in Tunisia • One Note Samba • Satin Doll • Take the "A" Train • Yardbird Suite • and more.

| | | |
|---|---|---|
| 00841438 | Flute | $10.95 |
| 00841439 | Clarinet | $10.95 |
| 00841440 | Alto Sax | $10.95 |
| 00841441 | Trumpet | $10.95 |
| 00841442 | Tenor Sax | $10.95 |
| 00841443 | Trombone | $10.95 |
| 00841444 | Violin | $10.95 |

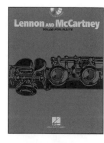

### Lennon and McCartney Solos

11 favorites: All My Loving • Can't Buy Me Love • Eleanor Rigby • The Long and Winding Road • Ticket to Ride • Yesterday • and more.

| | | |
|---|---|---|
| 00841542 | Flute | $10.95 |
| 00841543 | Clarinet | $10.95 |
| 00841544 | Alto Sax | $10.95 |
| 00841545 | Tenor Sax | $10.95 |
| 00841546 | Trumpet | $10.95 |
| 00841547 | Horn | $10.95 |
| 00841548 | Trombone | $10.95 |
| 00841549 | Violin | $10.95 |
| 00841625 | Viola | $10.95 |
| 00841626 | Cello | $10.95 |

### Movie & TV Themes

12 favorite themes: A Whole New World • Where Everybody Knows Your Name • Moon River • Theme from Schindler's List • Theme from Star Trek® • You Must Love Me • and more.

| | | |
|---|---|---|
| 00841452 | Flute | $10.95 |
| 00841453 | Clarinet | $10.95 |
| 00841454 | Alto Sax | $10.95 |
| 00841455 | Tenor Sax | $10.95 |
| 00841456 | Trumpet | $10.95 |
| 00841457 | Trombone | $10.95 |
| 00841458 | Violin | $10.95 |

### Sound of Music

9 songs: Climb Ev'ry Mountain • Do-Re-Mi • Edelweiss • The Lonely Goatherd • Maria • My Favorite Things • Sixteen Going on Seventeen • So Long, Farewell • The Sound of Music.

| | | |
|---|---|---|
| 00841582 | Flute | $10.95 |
| 00841583 | Clarinet | $10.95 |
| 00841584 | Alto Sax | $10.95 |
| 00841585 | Tenor Sax | $10.95 |
| 00841586 | Trumpet | $10.95 |
| 00841587 | Horn | $10.95 |
| 00841588 | Trombone | $10.95 |
| 00841589 | Violin | $10.95 |
| 00841590 | Viola | $10.95 |
| 00841591 | Cello | $10.95 |

### Worship Solos

11 top worship songs: Come, Now Is the Time to Worship • Draw Me Close • Firm Foundation • I Could Sing of Your Love Forever • Open the Eyes of My Heart • Shout to the North • and more.

| | | |
|---|---|---|
| 00841836 | Flute | $12.95 |
| 00841837 | Oboe | $12.95 |
| 00841838 | Clarinet | $12.95 |
| 00841839 | Alto Sax | $12.95 |
| 00841840 | Tenor Sax | $12.95 |
| 00841841 | Trumpet | $12.95 |
| 00841842 | Horn | $12.95 |
| 00841843 | Trombone | $12.95 |
| 00841844 | Violin | $12.95 |
| 00841845 | Viola | $12.95 |
| 00841846 | Cello | $12.95 |

0506